Lima built M1b 6783 takes on water at the Northumberland, Pa. mainline water column. June, 1956.

I REMEMBER PENNSY

by Don Wood

Where it all began . . .

For Rita and my girls . . .

Library of Congress Catalog Card Number: 73-80683

I REMEMBER PENNSY. Copyright 1973 by W. Don Wood. All rights reserved. No part of this book may be used or reproduced in any manner whatsoever without written permission of the author, except in the case of brief quotations used in reviews. Published by Audio-Visual Designs, P.O. Box 24, Earlton, New York 12058.

Printed in the United States of America by Compton Press, Inc., Morristown, New Jersey.

First Printing   September 1973
Second Printing   September 1974

2-10-0 4619 at Shamrock, Pa. on the Shamokin Branch.

Contents

Foreward	7
The New York Division	11
The New York & Long Branch	27
Philadelphia, PRSL, Wilmington & Baltimore	59
Color Photo Supplement	73
Harrisburg, Enola-Rockville	79
Along the Susquehanna	103
The Old Middle Division	119
Altoona & West	143
LCL (Less than Chapter Lots!)	159
Acknowledgments	167

Foreward...

THE photographs in this book depict the Pennsylvania Railroad in disguised descent. In the years following World War II, years when Don Wood was at PRR lineside with his camera, the system was not in its noontide of influence or usefulness. It had ceased to refer to itself as The Standard Railroad of the World. The westward tide of catenary had stopped for good in Harrisburg. The locomotive testing plant in Altoona was still. The great halls of Penn and 30th Street and Union no longer were scrubbed. The longest continuous dividend record in American history remained intact, but the annual payout had dropped to as little as 25 cents.

A measure of the railroad's former greatness is the fact that the human eye and the camera lens either seldom saw or safely ignored the arteriosclerosis of the Pennsy. In the obstinate refusal of steam to leave the property, we saw evidence of the system's heritage of independence and size. In the intruding ranks of E's and F's, sharks and C-Liners — yes, and GG1's with simplified single stripes and enormous keystones — we thought we saw the rebirth of the railroad assuring that it would remain the biggest, would ever cast the decisive vote on the AAR board.

For those who witnessed Pennsy, this pictorial will serve as record and reminder. More important, however, Don Wood's pictures will attest to both new and unborn generations that such an extraordinary institution as the PRR did indeed exist and will evidence the style of its operation.

Pennsy was (oh, the depression caused by that past tense!) different. Different in detail (keystone-shaped whistle signs), different in decor (tuscan-red passenger equipment), different in design (Belpaire boilers). In an earlier season, Pennsy was different because it was better in terms such as strength of car construction, weight of rail, standardization of motive power, capacity of terminals. In a later season, Pennsy was simply different (take the case of a mechanical department chieftain who studied with interest a builder's proposal for a new electric only to sweep the blueprint from his desk when he was informed that such a locomotive had been built for a subsidiary of the New York Central).

Pennsy was huge. What other railroad operated four tracks wide across the mountains, or carried more coal than any of the Pocahontas Region lines, or dominated an industrial complex the size of Pittsburgh. Pennsy was so huge that we were obliged to identify its engines by class rather than by number series — and not only because of the perversity of a system which strung out the road numbers of a set of 81 identical engines from 13 to 6513. Even in its decline, when it was just going through the motions, Pennsy was big enough to sustain Baldwin in the road diesel business; to create a national piggyback car pool; and unhappily, to shape Eastern ratemaking policy.

Now — and this is the point of this pictorial — the Pennsylvania Railroad managed to be different

and huge *and* engaging. Oh, there were those train-watchers who disparaged Pennsy for its admitted arrogance or its atypical locomotion; but I suggest that in their heart of hearts even these folk were moved by a brace of K4's coming to grips with the *Liberty Limited* out of Englewood or by a squat B6 shifter parting weeds on light iron in Jersey.

I am glad that the big system attracted a photographer with the enthusiasm, the energy, and the skill of Don Wood. PRR deserved no less. Indeed, after the collapse of the railroad's once peerless publicity force, the photographic record of the Pennsy in the region of its highest density of multiple track and traffic would be tragically lacking if Don, boy and man, had not so assiduously monitored the property. His work brackets an extraordinary — and as it turned out, the final — chapter of PRR history. His photos portray Pennsy from the time the weary giant emerged from the 1941-1945 war (surely the road's wartime role was its all-time contribution to America) to the hour it lost its identity in an unhappy, ill-fated merger with its arch rival. In retrospect, PRR's position-light signals were set at angled caution from 1945 on, but many of the illustrations in this book show otherwise. They depict traffic tides that recalled steam from storage; the influx of hundreds upon hundreds of diesels of diverse make and model; and the innovation that included Aerotrain, experimental electrics, piggyback, import-ore trains, a stainless-steel *Congressional*, and finally, the Metroliners.

In that season Pennsy was soft light and roast beef in the twin-unit diner of the *Broadway*, hammering Pacifics on the New York & Long Branch, awesome 4-8-2's with lengthy trains on the Middle Division, the incomparable GG1 in varied attire on varied consists, the smoke and shops of Altoona, and the uncountable other impressions and vistas of a magnificent transportation property thrust against its will into a time zone with which it ultimately could not cope.

I Remember Pennsy: the title is Don's and it is a good one. But it goes for all of us for whom the keystone always will imply a railroad rather than a commonwealth or a bridge.

David P. Morgan

TRAINS Magazine
Milwaukee, Wis.
May 1973

30

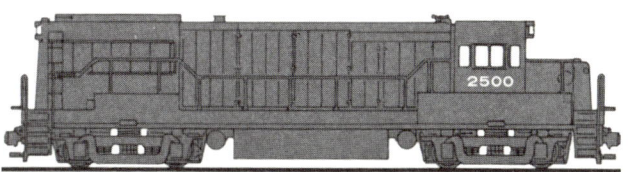

Following pages: K4 Pacifics 3751 and 3880 on the South Amboy, N.J. ready track, Midnight; September 12, 1957.

7

GG1 4900 leads Florida-bound "Silver Meteor" through curve at Menlo Park, N.J. August, 1954.

Chapter I

The New York Division

It's Saturday morning, September 18, 1954. The place: Newark, N.J. You're part of a pulsating crowd . . . a crowd of camera toting, engineer cap-wearing, steam hungry individuals that presses ever closer to the painted safety lines guarding track 2 of Newark's high level station. The clock overhead indicates 8:55 A.M. The familiar, echoing voice of the train caller is plainly audible over the din of the bustling mainline station: "Special train for Atlantic City now arriving track 2 . . .". The rest is lost in the clamor of a departing Hudson & Manhattan tube train a few tracks over.

Then suddenly you hear it: the unmistakable sound of steam . . . she's just over the Passaic River bridge, guardian of the east end of the station. Soon the high level platform will shake gently as she glides past . . . "I'll bet they gave us a K4" the young fellow in back of me volunteered. "No, it's an E6" I said assuredly, with ever so much a trace of know it all afluency. "In fact, if I know my engines, she sounds like the 460". He stood there, countenance transfixed in disbelieving awe, the puzzled "how can you tell?" look in his eyes.

I patted the letter in my coat pocket lovingly. It was from New York Division Superintendent Park M. Roeper granting permission to visit the Meadows (Kearny) enginehouse to photograph the servicing of the steam locomotive that would power the special train on the morning of September 18. My first port of call that A.M. was the Meadows Terminal where E6s 460, the last built of the 83 unit fleet of 4-4-2's, had indeed been assigned to the special run.

She was almost upon us now. As her bright red and gold keystone number plate swung into view, tension mounted rapidly. Flash bulbs began to pop and the excitement was reaching to encompass all within sight, sound, or smelling distance of this rare bird of a locomotive. It all culminated as she drifted by — bell sounding, generator whining and pops sizzling at the point of lift-off! Behind her low side tank were a baggage car and eight tuscan red P70 coaches. Precisely at nine two tugs on the communication cord signaled departure. The great Atlantic moved out. It marked the last time an E6 would ever visit Newark Station. Talk about memories . . . why, it was just 25 years before that this very locomotive literally flew through Newark with the legendary "Lindbergh Special" carrying films of the aviator's triumphant return to the U.S. after his epoch-making solo flight across the Atlantic in 1927.

Many other memories of the New York Division still burn brightly — the night aboard Piggybacker TT1 from Meadows to Chicago while on assignment for Editor Dave Morgan at TRAINS Magazine, the maiden runs of GM's snappy Aerotrain and Budd's tubular "Keystone", flawless GG1 electrics wheeling the "Broadway" and "General" at 85 per and P5's in the twilight of their careers hauling unbelievable tonnage. One of the last big thrills had to be the K4 Pacifics that still found their way to mainline iron between Jersey City and Union tower, Rahway. Here they would drop off the main line and head for the security that the end of the "wire" at South Amboy would bring almost into 1958!

The "Morning Congressional" behind GG1 4878 near "Snake Hill" between Newark and Bergen Hill Tunnels. View from front of MP54 MU car headed for Newark.

Pennsylvania Station, Newark, in the late fifties.

"Special train for Atlantic City, now arriving track . . ." Last time in Newark for an E6s Atlantic — September 18, 1954, 8:55 AM. No. 460, last built of the famous 83 unit fleet.

Newark Station on the mainline played host to steam right until the K4's were replaced on the NY&LB in late '57. Here, K4sa 612 leads "The Broker" in August of 1957.

A Philadelphia local slips out of Penn Station, Newark, behind pin-striped GG1 4935 in August, 1955.

GG1 power for Piggybacker TT1 is about to run around the TOFC's cabin and head for the front end! Meadows (Kearny) N.J. terminal.

TT1's conductor checks his waybills by kerosene lamp as the piggyback hot-shot rolls out of Meadows terminal.

Special train headed by Baldwin passenger "Shark" 5777 at Meadows terminal while PRR brass and shippers look over new "Truc-Train" facilities. The Pullman car behind the engine is "Henry S. Spang".

Looking over the new crane at Meadows terminal, 1961.

K4sa 612 was the regularly assigned power for "The Broker". For many months in '56-'57, this train represented the last steam passenger run that touched mainline tracks anywhere on the system. Action here is pushing 70 MPH a few miles west of Waverly Yard, Newark. September, 1957.

New Brunswick — New York local MU pulls out of the North Elizabeth station on a brassy hot afternoon in 1954. Note the relatively rare head end equipment in this consist.

GG1 4871 panned through Elizabeth, N.J., westbound.

Maiden westbound run of GM's "Aerotrain" finds the light-weight passing a GG1 powered train at Elizabeth station. She made the New York — Pittsburgh round trip daily for better than six months during 1956.

Another light-weight, Budd's tubular "Keystone" carried its own generator car behind the GG1. This is westbound action on the big curve at Elizabeth, N.J.

Alco FA2's in A-B-B-A lash-up under the wire at Elizabeth, heading for Waverly yard. A limited heads west on the "S" curve at right rear. You could always count on Pennsy to supply the unexpected!

They were called the workhorses of the electric fleet, and you can see why as box cabs 4715 and 4723 hum through North Elizabeth with tonnage for Enola yard. All units were retired by 1965.

It's January, 1968 and the photo of GG1's 4856 & 4853 with a train of loaded auto racks turned out to be my last PRR photo before the ill-fated merger with New York Central. Menlo Park, N.J.

The "Keystone" whips westbound through Colonia behind well maintained GG1 4874. This was the first trip for the new Budd-built train in 1956. The glory years were not yet behind.

"The Broker" of Woodbridge Wreck fame, this time behind the once streamlined 3678, has dropped off the mainline at Union interlocking, Rahway, and is now on the Perth Amboy & Woodbridge en route to the New York and Long Branch. A New York bound mainliner zips overhead behind the ever present GG1. July, 1955.

Chapter II
The New York and Long Branch

As the longest chapter in this volume you might expect that the NY&LB was a super division or major main line somewhere within the confines of the giant Pennsylvania System rather than the 38.4 mile commuter line that the Pennsy shared with co-owner Jersey Central. What could possibly eat up 32 pages of 168? Only the "Long Branch Route": the final stamping grounds for Pennsy's legendary K4s Pacifics. Pennsy catenary ended just on the outskirts of South Amboy and for years GG1 electrics traded places with the rakish 4-6-2's and vice-versa. As diesels gradually took over mainline passenger trains west of Harrisburg, Pa., untold numbers of K4's were sent to storage or scrap. With new diesels extremely scarce and costly in the fifties, Pennsy figured: "What better way to run out the miles on the K4's than the NY&LB?".

That was not the sole reasoning. Long Branch trains, especially in the summer months, were running as heavy as 15 P70 coaches . . . enough to require two diesel units per train . . . something PRR was not about to indulge in for a commuter line. Endless numbers of the big Pacifics arrived and departed the Long Branch service between 1953 and late 1957 — when PRR dropped the fires on steamers system wide — the period of time I was fortunate enough to have photographed the line. Groups of Pacifics built years apart and by different builders worked side by side and quite often doubleheaded! There was Juniata, Baldwin, and Altoona Works* builders plates spanning 13 years.

The NY&LB, serving the North Jersey Coast, was unique in many other ways. Consider 78 crossings at grade level along 38 miles of line, and you begin to realize that the engineer rarely got his hand off the whistle cord! Want stack music? The 16 or 17 station stops were so close that an engineer would hardly get a roll on 'em when he would have to brake for the next stop. Mix in 3 bascule lift bridges along the route and you begin to get an idea of what railroading was like on "The Branch". When E7's first began to infiltrate in the spring of '56, continual starting and stopping with long trains resulted in overheating, causing overload circuits to cut in and disable the units.

Despite all the stops, there was room for some lively running. The raceway was between Matawan and Red Bank if no stop was scheduled at Middletown. Speeds between 65 and 70 were recorded, despite the fact that the line was signaled for a maximum of 60. K4's were equipped with recorders and speed control apparatus that some enginemen were able to override. The seven mile run between South Amboy and Matawan was also a good spot for "stepping through the dew".

So, you see, it was really very easy to be swept up in the goings-on of the New York & Long Branch in the fifties. K4's and GG1's went off and on the point of better than thirty trains a day. In the summer, racetrack extras out of Exchange Place, Jersey City, with steam all the way, made the dust fly up and down the line! Another aspect of the operation was just as noteworthy; I speak of the railroaders who worked the line . . . PRR and CNJ crews, the South Amboy enginehouse gang that kept the old K4's in steam, and down by the station at South Amboy . . . switchman Bill Sexton and the crossing watchman at John Street, a Black man they called "Logan". Their tales of railroading on the Long Branch are never to be forgotten, especially the descriptions of engineer Hughie McCabe and the Milk Train. The New York and Long Branch . . . A subject to return to sometime . .

*Juniata Shops took the name Altoona Works in 1928.

win built K4 5412 on NY&LB train 709 at Morgan, N.J. in 1955.

South Amboy, N.J. ....

K4 5471 drifts into South Amboy station with N.Y. train. GG1 that will couple on here is seen at right rear near MU coach yard. July. 1954.

South Amboy engine terminal ready track line up in July, 1954.
From the left: 5406, 1453, 3884.

General View: South Amboy engine terminal in 1954.

South Amboy Silhouette: 3880 backlighted by engine terminal lights in this dramatic after dark shot in 1957.

3752 and 646 shake hands in front Baldwin BP20 unit. Not many photos h ever depicted PRR locos with solid dr coupler pilots coupled nose to n

K4 5439 pokes her modernized front end out of South Amboy enginehouse in September, 1957.

K4's 3751 and 3880 in stunning night
portrait at South Amboy in September, 1957.

A Rare Bird . . . passenger "Sharknose" 5782
in pin-stripe attire at South Amboy.

Experimental class E2c from BLH and Westinghouse. These C-C, AC-DC rectifier type locos were the forerunners of the new E44 class locos now in service on PC.

Beautifully conditioned Alco FA & FB2's await assignment at South Amboy, N.J.

win Sharknose freighters in A-B on the
track.

Down by the Station ....

Engine change at South Amboy station — a ritual performed 30 times a day in both directions. Above: Double headed K4's are cut off and move toward engine terminal. Below: GG1 4910 backs down on train and will continue run into New York City.

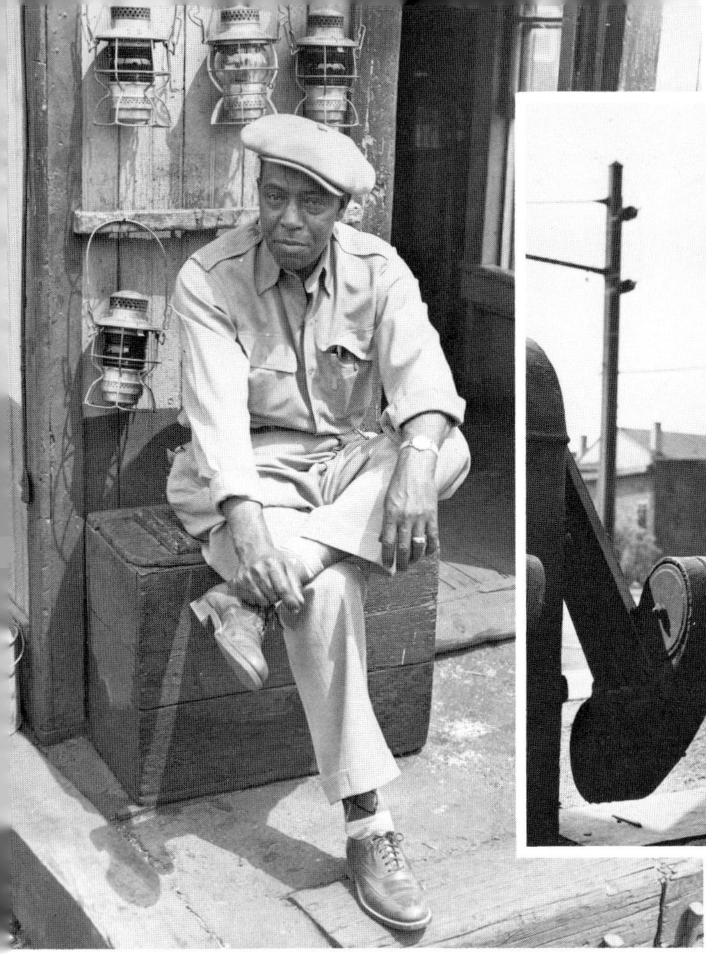

Crossing watchman "Logan" (above) spun yarns of railroad lore and nostalgia while we sat around his coal fired pot-bellied stove in the John Street shanty. His tales of the late Hughie McCabe and his hair raising feats with the milk train are never to be forgotten. The old switchman, Bill Sexton (above, right), captivated railfans young and old with his tales of railroading on the old NY&LB.

Alco PA's under the able hand of Zeke Schible back down on train 787 one Sunday afternoon in 1957.

An Ominous Foreboding

Spotless E7 5879 — an ominous foreboding — takes train 711 out of South Amboy station. This was the first PRR diesel powered run on the NY&LB. April, 1956.

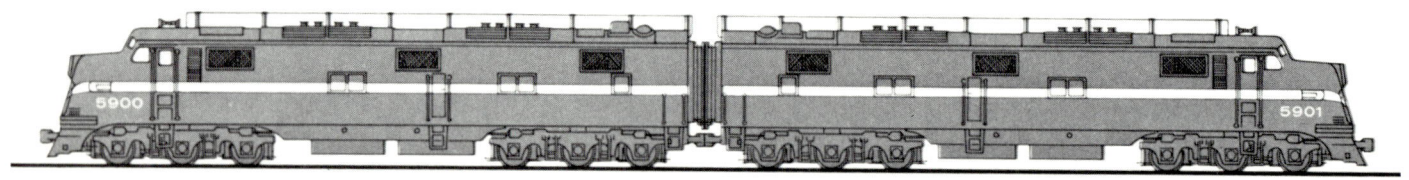

Once streamlined 3678 hammers hard out of South Amboy for points on the North Jersey Coast. April, 1956.

After uneventful first run, E7 5879 arrives back at South Amboy station. Ground crew prepares to make cut off.

Main Line Meet ....

A pair of mainline meets on the NY&LB just south of South Amboy. Above, 3884 races away from the camera as 5412 comes on. Right, 5471 comes at the camera as seen from the fireman's side of 1139! Both photos in the same location — Roll 'em!!

Would you believe K4 No. 16 on the NY&LB in August of '55? Here, she drifts into South Amboy on the head end of No. 734 from Bay Head. This old K4 was the only two digit Pacific I ever ran across, and this was the only occasion!

3884 backs down to train as GG1 4870 waits in the clear.

K4s 5473 rattles the catenary as she blasts out of South Amboy with Sunday only train 787. November, 1955.

Old friend 612 again; this time on train 717 out of Amboy. The catenary tells the story: AC MOTOR STOP.

Above: Altoona built 1453 awaits special train at South Amboy. Below: The late Harry Snow is at the throttle as 1453 heads for an Asbury Park convention with an all Pullman consist!

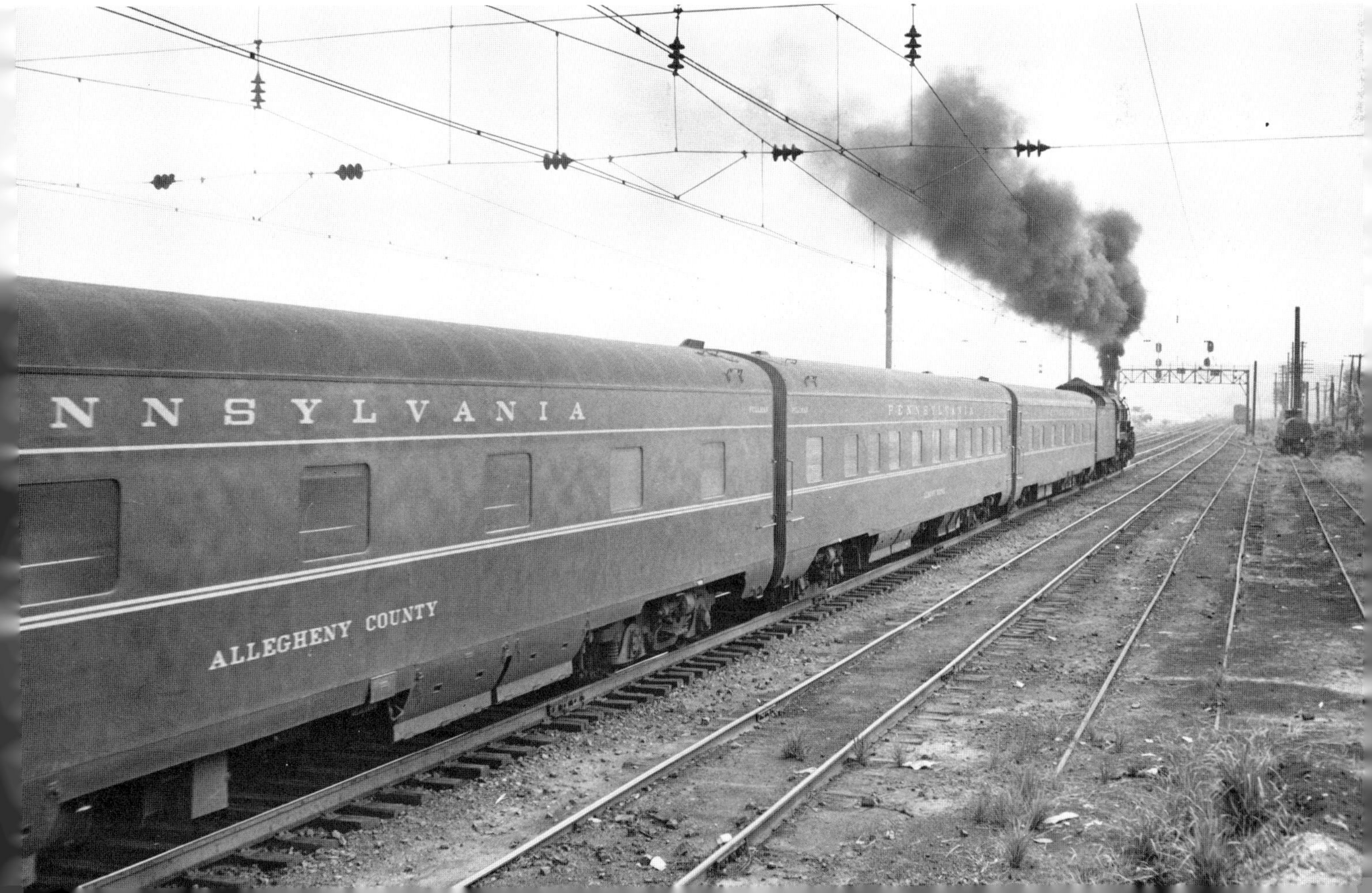

A view from the top — K4 830 blasts up Matawan Hill with train 786 in August, 1957.

K4 646 roars under N.J. route 35 at Morgan Station with train 787!

3751 & 1361 on the move up Matawan Hill at milepost 6. That's fireman Ferdinand Norman leaning out of 3751's cab. Train 784 was usually doubleheaded on Sunday as part of power transfer move.

Roaring up the shoreline of Raritan Bay with a gusto of old are K4's 3884 and 3752 in September, 1954. View is from route 35 bridge. Note smashboard at back of signal on the right

It's 6 degrees above zero at Matawan, N.J. in January of 1956 as the 612 comes at the camera in an awesome action display sequence. By the way, train number is lucky 711, not that it matters!

One of the last built of the 425 unit fleet of K4s Pacifics. No. 5497 accelerates train 726 north over the Shrewsbury Avenue crossing at Red Bank in 1953.

The old Speed Graphic barely got back inside the open-window P70 coach before opposing train with 3678 on the point slammed by. North Long Branch, 1954.

A favorite of mine on several counts: engine 1361, which I was priveleged to run at one time and is now preserved at Horseshoe Curve; the engineer on the run, a personal friend, the late Harry Snow; and the train, a Monmouth Park extra, is raising the dust at Matawan station in Matawan Boro . . . my current residence!

3752 with four car weekend train at Manasquan in spring of 1956. Train 717 is headed for Bay Head Jct.

K4 5409 booms across Shark River Inlet bridge with train 735. Belmar, N.J., July, 1954.

You can almost smell that invigorating salt air as you watch a southbound K4-powered train rumble over Manasquan River bridge at the Brielle Yacht Basin.

A bit of backlighted drama as double slotted 4-6-2's roar northward over Manasquan River Inlet bridge in 1954.

3806 races for the metropolis after crossing Manasquan River bridge. Note small auxiliary headlight above the Keystone number plate.

612 and 3751 roll toward Point Pleasant from Bay Head with Sunday train 784 on a cold February day.

Old 5417 on sand as she lifts nine cars of train 717 south from Point Pleasant station. Crossing is at Arnold Avenue; the late Harry Rayes is at the throttle.

Arnold Avenue crossing again as 5351 heads into the morning sun with train 709.

Bay Head Jct., N.J., southernmost terminus of NY&LB, finds 3 K4's and CNJ Baldwin "double-ender" laying over for the weekend. July, 1954.

A most memorable day . . . July 11, 1954. A fan trip behind Jersey Central 4-6-0 Camelback 774 stops at Bay Head Jct. while fans visit with PRR K4's that are tied up for the weekend.

Bay head Jct. afforded many opportunities for shooting the unusual. Case in point: K4's 5439 and 3750 flank passenger "Shark" 5783.

Bay Head motive power line up in winter of 1956 featured K4's 5372, 1361, and 5348.

Ferdinand Norman, stoking 5367, and Johnny Maxwell on 1453 make smoke for the camera on a cold March day in 1956. Train 784 is just out of Bay Head Jct., northbound.

A Pennsy classic: E6s 4-4-2 1600 in the Camden, N.J. roundhouse in 1954.

Chapter III
Philadelphia, PRSL, Wilmington & Baltimore

You might imagine that Philadelphia, being the hot bed of PRR operations, would have occupied much of my time in the years of shooting "The Standard Railroad of the World". Nothing could be farther from the truth! Philly definitely was not where the action was in the fifties . . . if your interest was to search out the remaining pockets of steam power. Across the Delaware, over in Camden, N.J., it was another story. Pennsylvania-Reading Seashore Lines were running the wheels off many a K4, L1, B6, H9 or 10 and even a few G5 Ten-Wheelers, along with the "Three Sisters" . . . the last active E6 Atlantics — 460, 645, and 1600! Other than several photos made at 30th Street Station in Philly on the occasion of the PRR's displaying the first E44 electric, a brief 1955 visit to the old 32nd Street enginehouse resulted in the only photography worth mentioning.

The G5's and E6's working commuter runs between Pemberton and Broadway Station in Camden certainly held the most interest in the mid-fifties. This does not mean that the peripatetic photographer would ignore the K4's and Reading G3's winding it up on the speedway between Camden and Atlantic City, just as in days long gone!

The Author may well be accused of having a hang-up where the E6 4-4-2 is concerned. Not quite true. Indeed, Gibbs' racer was held in high esteem as were most of the PRR locomotives created on the boards at Philadelphia or Altoona. It's simply that the breed was getting so rare that finding one in service was cause to shake even the most temperate of individuals! Shaken I was on the Sunday morning I chanced upon old friend 460 sitting adjacent to an honest-to-gosh gas-electric Doodlebug at Pemberton. If you have any trouble getting the picture . . . turn to page 62 . . . it's there waiting for you!!!

"CTE EA" . . . were locomotive assignment classifications appearing on either end of the pilot beam of PRR locomotives. In this instance, the stenciling indicated a locomotive belonging to the East Altoona pool that was assigned to the Camden Terminal enginehouse. In charge of this roundhouse in the early fifties was a genial man named Dale Cherry. His enginehouse was the only one I ever saw that was kept in a beautiful state of whitewash . . . inside . . . live steam not withstanding! It was in this roundhouse that the photo of E6 1600 on the opposite page was shot in the fall of 1954, along with a photo of G5 5720 which ranks in the top three of my own all time favorite list. Thank you, Dale Cherry . . . wherever you may be.

Just south of Philadelphia, in Delaware, lies Pennsy's sprawling Wilmington Shops. The road's entire electric fleet get class repairs and major rebuilding there. An all time memory was registered in early March of 1960 while once again on assignment for TRAINS Magazine; Editor Morgan was doing a huge layout on the GG1 electric in an upcoming issue. The groundwork was laid with PRR and I arrived at the shops to find them wheeling out old number 4811, freshly painted with the new solid stripe motif and looking like she was fresh from GE. After shooting up a storm on 4811, the shop foreman asked if I would like to try my hand at the throttle!!! I ran her up and down the yard lead a couple of times. That topped even the K4's I used to help hostle around the yard at South Amboy!!! A tour of the shop bay followed with gratifying results photographically. GG1's, P5's, and even the R1 were in various stages of undress, presenting a scene that had to be seen to be believed.

The last photo in this chapter shows Pennsylvania Station, Baltimore. One of my favorite structures on the PRR, I like to call it "Pennsy's Acropolis" because of its obvious Greco-Roman architectural influence and the way it seems to sit above and dominate its surroundings. A true landmark in Baltimore.

The first of PRR's new E44 rectifiers unveiled at press conference at 30th Street Station in Philadelphia. June, 1960.

New E44 electric with special display train at 30th Street Station.

GG1 4921 holds the outside iron as she overtakes eastbound freight at Morrisville, Pa. in the summer of 1954.

An early March snowstorm blankets Thorndale, Pa. as FF2's 6 and 4, recently acquired from Great Northern, do their thing in not unusual weather conditions for these engines!

PRSL - Camden .... Atlantic City ....

This photograph ranks right up at the top of my own all time Pennsy (or any other road, for that matter) favorite list. Just coming upon this scene at Pemberton, N.J. was a happening never to be forgotten. E6 460 of course, is of a long and illustrious career, while the gas-electric "Doodlebug" is just downright rare in the PRR scheme of things!

The classic lines of Pennsy's great racer, the E6 4-4-2, are graphically illustrated in these two shots at Atlantic City featuring the "Lindbergh" Atlantic, No. 460.

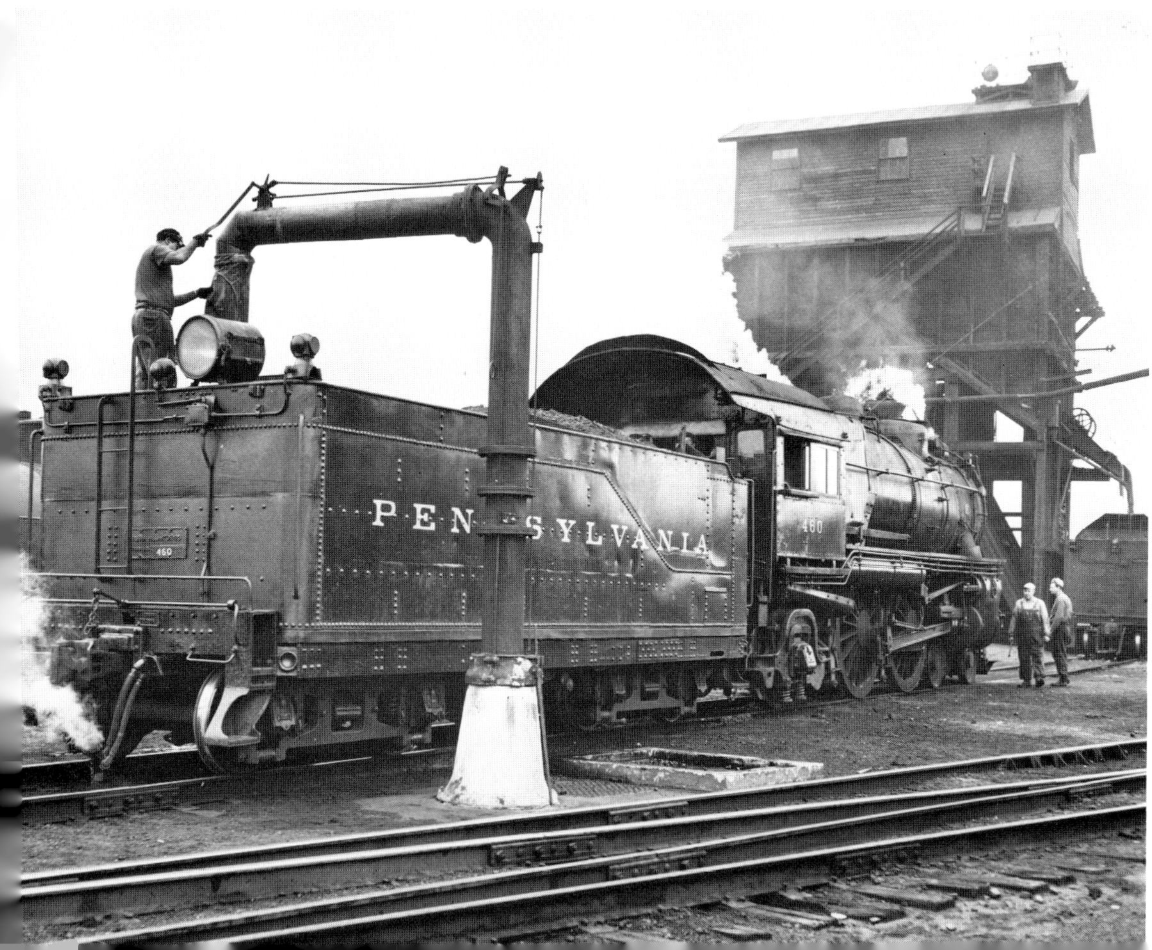

It's bitter cold at Camden Terminal as B6sb 1733 takes water. Pennsy's fleet of sturdy 0-6-0's were popular shifters in and around Camden and Philadelphia.

B6 goats ready for day's work out of Camden. The tender at right belongs to a Reading G3 Pacific.

Camden Terminal Enginehouse was a pure wonder in the mid-fifties. On any given day, a visitor with a camera could find and shoot K4's, E6's, G5's, H9 & 10's, B6 and A5 shifters, and L1 mikes, not to mention Reading power. G5 5720 and a B6 are serviced in this 1956 photo.

K4's 5022 and 5495 roll past Atlantic Tower, Atlantic City, to pick up race track train for Garden State Park. September, 1954.

The Three Sisters

Last of the 4-4-2 E6S Atlantics

460 at Atlantic City
1600 at Camden
645 at Pemberton

Wilmington Shops

Running gear from GG1 4883 sits alongside carbody while heavy, class repairs are underway at the Wilmington, Delaware Shops.

Rare birds-eye view of sprawling Wilmington shops where most heavy work on PRR's electric fleet was undertaken. View from traveling overhead crane.

GG1's and P5's in the shop bay at Wilmington.

Grimy & Tired

Shopping GG1

t Wilmington

Shiny & New

Pennsylvania Station - Baltimore ....

Pennsy's "Acropolis" !!

It's the 3747 again... this time bearing down on the Cliffwood Avenue crossing with Sunday afternoon train 787. Children in the station shelter cover their ears against the big Pacific's onslaught!

Train 787 on a different Sunday finds peripatetic 3752 blasting away from South Amboy after taking over from GG1.

Baldwin built 5406 on the "trailer track" near Connover's Cove, South Amboy. Steam K4's usually waited here for GG1-powered trains from New York.

K4s 3747 at South Amboy engine terminal on a cold and windy Sunday morning in March, 1956.

John St. crossing, South Amboy . . . A rare pin-striped Baldwin "Sharknose" diesel has just backed onto train 711, while GG1 that brought the train from New York moves away. The "Shark" seems as far removed now as the K4s!

Engines 830 and 1983 have just crossed Cheesequake Creek bridge at Morgan Station on the last leg of the journey from Bay Head to South Amboy. Train is No. 782.

I'll never forget this shot if I live to be 200! It marked the last time I would ever see a live Pennsy 2-10-0, and the event occurred on the same Saturday in September, 1957 that the Russians orbited their first Sputnik! Speak about paradox!

K4 5439 poses in the doorway of South Amboy enginehouse. The time was late on two counts: The 1:30 AM photo time plus the curtain coming down on the career of the engine herself, as well as for all Pennsy steam. The end was less than a month away, as this was October, 1957.

Alco's freight version of their famous PA passenger units: FA2 and FB1 pose outside Enola diesel shop in 1956.

The "Reynolds Wrap" or the "Lionel", if you will, swings west off Rockville Bridge on the way from New York to Pittsburgh. Peter's Mountain forms the impressive backdrop.

GG1 4919 waits at South Amboy for arrival of train from Bay Head.

And Now .... to the Land of the "Mountains" ....

Chapter IV
Harrisburg, Enola-Rockville

Alas! Harrisburg in the fifties suffered much the same fate in my eyes as did Philadelphia. I like to refer to it, albeit unfairly, as much ado over not very much, especially when one considers the spectacle that unfolded there every day in the "Glory Years". Oh, yes, the GG1's still moved the Blue Ribbon Fleet in and out of the old multi-peaked trainshed with what amounted to boring regularity. The difference was in the motive power that flung the Tuscan Heritage westward. K4's and T1's powered their last trains in 1952, with only a stand-by 4-6-2 available in a pinch at the beginning of 1953. So, while there was much activity with EMD E7's and 8's, and to a much lesser extent Alco PA's and Baldwin Sharknose power, the transient photographer could not tarry for long, since heaven lay almost directly across the Susquehanna!!! Heaven in this instance was sprawling Enola Yard, at that time the largest classification point on the Pennsy. I do not know what significance can be attached to the fact that Enola when spelled backwards becomes "Alone". One thing is for sure: if you were a dedicated follower of the Tuscan Order you could never be alone at Enola, for this was the "magic garden" of the fifties. Better than 8,000 cars a day in both directions rolled through the huge facility, and to move that kind of traffic you needed MOTIVE POWER!!! GG1's and P5's moved most of the tonnage to the east and south while steam and diesel shared the duties to the west and north.

Right in the midst of this mind-boggling plant was a fantastic full circle roundhouse that was almost as big as the celebrated Altoona facility. A tremendous diesel shop stood adjacent to the steam structure, and beyond that, a monumental four track concrete coaling stage with all the accessories: inspection and ash-pit tracks, water columns, and the like. Big barrelled 2-10-0's, some with tanks longer than the engine, shoved long lines of cars over the east and westbound hump leads, while spunky H9 2-8-0's scurried about making up trains and digging out incorrectly classified cars. Over on the westbound ready tracks were clusters of the beloved, keystone festooned, Belpaire-boilered 4-8-2 M1's awaiting the call to duty, along with an occasional I1 2-10-0 or L1 Mike. In 1955, when 50% of the trains dispatched from Enola to the Middle and Susquehanna Divisions were steam powered, the balance of assignments were shared by EMD F3's and 7's, FP7's, and early GP7's while Alco FA's and Baldwin Sharks picked up the slack. GP and SD9's began arriving in 1956 and along with Alco RSD15's started cutting into both steam and cab unit operations. The relatively short time all were working together afforded the photographer who did not deliberately shun the diesel some great photographic possibilities! Throw in the leasing in 1956 of a dozen or so Reading T1 4-8-4's and you had a melting pot of power unrivaled anywhere . . . why, they even let L1 2-8-2's out over Rockville Bridge in Enola-Harrisburg transfer service!

Speaking of Rockville Bridge, the action in both directions over the world's largest stone arch span was something you just had to witness. Camping at the west end, or Marysville side, you might see freight coming down the Susquehanna Division and over the bridge into Enola. While this was going on, trains off the Middle Division in both directions would be held until the first train cleared. Before the two previously held trains could clear, northbound tonnage out of Enola and bound for the Susquehanna Division would be held until the Middle Division trains cleared. In the meantime, traffic going directly in and out of Enola to and from the Middle Division passed continually in front of you. If the hour was in the late morning, you may have been lucky enough to see GM's Aerotrain slip through all this traffic while en route to Pittsburgh! Carefully place the motive power picture outlined earlier into the Rockville action just completed, shake lightly, sprinkle generously with cinders, add a little diesel fuel to taste, simmer slowly in your mind for a few seconds, then simply turn the page and watch the story unfold the way I most vividly remember it . . . through the perpetuality of the filmed image!

2-10-0 4519 crosses Rockville Bridge on the way to Enola yard with tonnage off the Susquehanna Division.

Harrisburg, Pa.

GG1's tied up at Harrisburg engine terminal waiting out Trainmen's strike in 1960. Note the steam era water columns visible through the coal wharf. The plug serving the track on the right is gigantic compared to the standard size job at the left. The big spout was needed to get over the side of those huge T1 Duplex tenders!

GG1 activity was always brisk at Harrisburg, with all westbound trains going to steam or diesel at this point and just reversing the procedure for eastbound movement.

GG1 4916 awaits arrival of eastbound passenger train at Harrisburg.

Enola Yard ....

Sprawling Enola yard showing service track area, the scene dominated by the big 360 degree roundhouse.

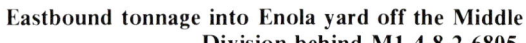

Eastbound tonnage into Enola yard off the Middle Division behind M1 4-8-2 6805.

Looking down on M1b 6762 at the west end of the yard.

L1s 6309 makes up transfer run for Harrisburg in Enola's westbound yards.

Chunky 2-8-0 8220 in odd below rail level view. Pennsy H9's and 10's were in service right up to steam's end on the big road.

M1b 6754 takes the low line by-pass around Enola (top right) and heads for Altoona with long string of empty hoppers.

proud ones . . . two of Pennsy's finest in steam pose
nola enginehouse. The M1 4-8-2's were regarded
the highest esteem in all echelons of the old PRR.

4-8-2 6755 eases off Enola turntable and into after bringing in freight off the Middle Division. roundhouse was razed early in 1968, but remains as the sole survivor of her class at the Penn vania State Museum at Strasb

Surprise!! Not many photographers were fortunate enough to shoot a K4s Pacific on Enola's big table, but as they say, the proof is in the seeing . . . 5439 heads for a berth in the 360 degree roundhouse in 1956.

As good a view as you are ever likely to see of the top side of a "Coast to Coast" tender: water scoop air cylinder, antenna, water hatches, dog house and coal bunker.

Enola at night. 2-8-2 6265 at left, and 4-8-2 6760 under the giant coal wharf in June of 1956.

A scene of happier times. The 4-8-2 has just delivered a coal train to the electrics at Harrisburg and is returning to Enola via Rockville Bridge. Here, we see her entering the west end of the huge yard before dropping the cabin car.

Brand new Alco DL-600B after arrival at Enola in June, 1956.

2-10-0 4408 and huge 210-F-84 tender headed to Harrisburg with N8 cabin to pick up empty hoppers for movement west.

M1b 6762 gets ready for run west to Altoona. The Susquehanna River provides the backdrop.

Three new GP9's lead solid block of reefers into Enola as an A-B-B-A lash-up of F7's heads west.

Williamsport tonnage behind Alco 8613 waits to cross Rockville Bridge, while westbound stock and refrigerator cars from the east stretch out behind M1b 6738's huge tank and all the way across the bridge and down the eastern bank of the Susquehanna.

Freight out of Renovo crosses Rockville Bridge behind 2-10-0 4644. She will tie up at Enola in less than 15 minutes.

Pennsy EMD F`s in A-B-A multiple lead long string of empties west-bound over Rockville Bridge.

L1 Mikado coming and going under bridge approaches with local freight.

FA2's out of Enola head onto Rockville Bridge with Susquehanna Division train destined for Renovo. November, 1955.

Fairbanks-Morse "C liners" head westbound empties out of Enola. Photo as seen from the bridge.

Over and under they go! Williamsport-Enola train EC2 on the top, while early version of TT1 heads west under Rockville Bridge leg.

Aerotrain at Rockville !!!

On the eastbound leg of the NY-Pittsburgh run, GM's Aerotrain makes a striking photo as she heads onto the world's longest stone arch bridge just after sunset. August, 1956.

Oft published photo of M1b 6761 heading out over Rockville Bridge with the "Buffalo Boxcar" is included here because the author feels that this volume of photographic memories of PRR would not be complete without it!

M1 6888 heads into morning sun and mist at Rockville. She will deliver her coal loads to waiting P5's at Harrisburg within the half hour.

Ice floes clog the Susquehanna River on
December 31, 1955, as M1b 6717 heads for
the Middle Division and Altoona.

M1b 6739 waits to cross Rockville Bridge
with eastbound coal.

I1 4243 poses in the house at Northumberland, Pa.

Chapter V

Along The Susquehanna

Let's assume that the tonnage out of Enola destined for the Susquehanna Division, which was held for Middle Division trains at Rockville Bridge in the last chapter, has just received a "proceed" indication. Engineer Wally Reader calls in his flag with five longs on the big 4-8-2's whistle. After a 20 or 30 second wait, two short blasts tell everyone that the daily except Sunday "Buffalo Boxcar" was about to get underway. On sand, and without ever so much a trace of slipping, M1b 6761 stretches out the slack and moves out over the bridge. 109 cars later, the N5c cabin, with the ever present trainphone antenna atop its full length, rolls by with a friendly wave from the rear platform. Across the river, the 4-8-2 is talking it up, her mile high exhaust moving almost as if by magic between the trees and foliage of the river and the huge backdrop offered by Peter's Mountain!

You want to sit and watch until the cabin is beyond the capability of your sight . . . but you know that old Pa. route 14 follows the railroad almost all of the way to Sunbury, and through some very scenic country. You dive into the venerable '53 Plymouth and take off for the five cent toll bridge at Duncannon that will take you across the Susquehanna and to route 14.

Wow!!! You're on route 11-15 in Duncannon which follows the Middle Division for several miles and the smokey haze ahead tells you something's doing. To stop or not to stop? That was the question! You stop. . . the moral: never look a gift (iron) horse in the mouth. You fly out of the auto with Graphic in hand as M1 6747 bears down on your location . . . but wait . . . the whistle from the rear . . . you look over your shoulder to glimpse hotshot PG-5 roaring west. But I'm getting ahead of myself . . . this is chapter 5, not 6, so let's pick up the chase on the other side of the river!

Racing ahead to a point you assume Wally Reader and the 6761 could not yet have reached, you bring all of your cunning and knowledge of train chasing into play. A close look at the track shows just a trace of discoloration from the early morning dew. A look north at a distant position light signal showed the vertical aspect: clear board! The "Buffalo Boxcar" had not yet been by. You have just determined that you're on the outskirts of Halifax, Pa. when the rapid stacatto exhaust is heard in the not too far off distance. You take up station on a gentle curve just as the high stepping Mountain breaks into view. Then you see it: possible disaster looms as, about 20 cars back, smoke is pouring from a hot journal. Did you ever try and give the old washout or big hole indication while you had a 4x5 Speed Graphic on your wrist? Wally got the message after he saw me hold two fingers to my nose. He acknowledged with two shorts on the whistle and shut off on 6761. They set out the hotbox at Halifax and Wally said to meet him at the Sunbury water stop. I was there as he expertly stopped the train, the hatch atop the "Coast to Coast" tender opposite the water column, without splitting the consist!

"Come on with me down to the house". Wally left his fireman with the engine to take on water while he walked a half block to his clean, simple home and announced to his charming wife that there would be a guest for dinner. The venison pot pie consumed that evening, to this day, evokes memories of whistles in the night . . . steam on the move . . . all about Wally Reader, M1b 6761, and the "Buffalo Boxcar".

Memories of the Susquehanna are so numerous that, in conclusion, I can only touch on a very few: the Mt. Carmel Ore Train for one. What a spectacle! The last of the great I1 Decapods working their guts out on the tortuous twisting line that ran between Sunbury and Mt. Carmel, south of Shamokin. 2-10-0's out of the Northumberland Pool, two fore and two aft, would leave "Nory" each morning with their heavy ore lading, their thundering exhausts reverberating across the Shamokin Valley, leaving no doubt of their intent to deliver the goods to the LV interchange at Mt. Carmel! If you were ever fortunate enough to partake of the aforementioned event, I think you might agree than an apt phrase to cover the happening could well be "Hell on the Hill"!

Speaking of Northumberland, the enginehouse there stabled, in addition to the 2-10-0's used on the ore train, 4-8-2's and 2-8-0's in mainline and yard service. The famous collection of PRR historical locomotives was also berthed there, and remained until 1968 when most of the collection was moved to the State Museum at Strasburg where it can be seen today. Could be that sometime in the future I will elaborate a bit more on the scenic area above Lock Haven and Jersey Shore, winding up at Renovo and Hyner Lookout . . .

Pennsy's mighty Mountain in full stride as seen pacing by auto on Pa. route 14 near Halifax. You can almost hear her "talking it up".

M1 6967 roars under bridge carrying Pa. route 14 over Shamokin Creek.

105

L1 Mike chuffs into yard at Renovo with freight off the Bald Eagle branch. No. 3277 escaped PRR's post war "beauty treatment" and wears her headlight as when built.

4-8-2 6940 shruggs off pelting rain as she rumbles east through Sunbury. Note her odd, welded, twelve wheel tank, probably off a K4 that had been re-equipped some years before.

Who will ever forget the memorable summer of 1956 when PRR, short of motive power, leased a batch of T1 4-8-4's from Reading? They were used mostly on Susquehanna Division trains. T1 2113 has Enola-bound tonnage out of Williamsport on the move just east of Sunbury.

Meet The 6783 ....

"Glamour Girl" 6783 blows for crossing near Dauphin on a rainy morning in May, 1956.

6783 has a good roll on 'em as she nears Rockville with train EC2. The big Mountain got the train at Williamsport.

FP7's in tuscan red and pinstripes on the move near Montandon, Pa. Freight out of Renovo is destined for Enola.

Freight out of Wilkes-Barre as seen from Montandon Tower. The green FP7 "A" unit is trailed by a passenger-equipped F7B which is decked out in tuscan and pinstripes! Train is Buffalo-bound.

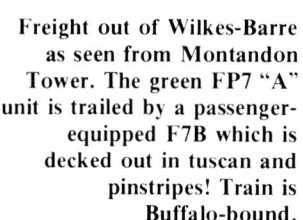

The Washington Express, train 570, rolls south through Northumberland behind E8 5835.

Alco FA2 and FB1 at Selinsgrove, Pa. on the way to Harrisburg. Note rare application of large Keystone decal on nose of lead unit. Most were half this size!

Northumberland, Pa. ....

Northumberland Passenger Station . . . an all brick and slate masterpiece erected in 1910!

Northumberland Engine Terminal lined 'em up this way in 1956. Second engine from left, H10 7688, is preserved in the Pennsylvania State Museum at Strasburg.

2-8-0 7688 again, 12 years later, in storage at Northumberland as part of PRR historical collection. Also shown are H6sb 2846 and the ever present E6s 460.

Stand Back . . . here com[es]
the "Mt. Carmel Ore Train["].
Winter action on t[he]
Shamokin Valley line ne[ar]
Weigh Scal[es.]

Helpers meet at Crowl on [the]
Shamokin Branch. All 2-10[-0's]
in ore train service w[ere]
based at Northumberl[and]
enginehou[se.]

I1s 1126 on the Shamokin Branch with the legendary
"Mt. Carmel Ore Train". Curve near Weigh Scales is
so sharp that second engine cannot be seen in this view.
Spring, 1956.

ngineer Barber rolls across Sunbury grade
ossing with the 4499 on the point of the
Mt. Carmel Ore Train".

Two big "Hippos" blast away from water stop at
Shamrock Tank in August of 1955. The hills were alive
with the sound of stack music!

g up for a day's work at "Nory", I1 4241
wo sisters are "marked up" for morning
un.

Chapter VI
The Middle Division

Only the mere mention of the Middle Division is enough to evoke nostalgic and wonderfully exciting, almost stereoptician-like images of the Pennsylvania Railroad of the past. I remember vividly my first visit to the Middle Division area. It was akin to the feeling that a Boy Scout Troop probably experienced when they came upon their first bit of Indian lore or found themselves exploring a trail that the guide said was the same one used three centuries ago by a tribe of local hostiles! So it was on the sunny fall day in 1953 when I climbed up the steep embankment at Duncannon just in time to lens M1 6898 roaring through. I was impressed enough to use the photo as the frontspiece for this chapter. I never saw 6898 again, but the parade of sisters that was to follow numbered in excess of 80 locomotives over five years!

The M1 — M1a 4-8-2's were my cup of tea. Beautifully balanced; long, lean, and powerful, the Mountains had everything . . . they said it all. Built originally to eliminate the doubleheading of passenger trains over Horseshoe Curve, their assignment changed as they appeared in greater numbers in the early thirties. Most, and eventually all, were to wind up in freight service. I was never fortunate enough to see an M1 head up a limited, but to see one winding it up through the Juniata River Valley with a hot-shot gave you some idea of her feats while hauling passenger trains. Through all the years in service, the M1 was inseperable from the Middle Division. She was used throughout the system, but recognized home grounds were the Middle and Susquehanna Divisions. Right up to the end of steam operations on the PRR, you could find 4-8-2's leaving Enola with tonnage trains, long after more sophisticated power had been retired.

Let's go back for a moment to the impending "Meet" at Duncannon as outlined in chapter 5: 6747 is "smoking it up" around the big "s" curve with coal headed for Harrisburg. That low, hoarse whistle from the rear spins you around just in time to glimpse 6921 roaring toward you with a long string of yellow reefers. Which train to shoot? 6747 is closer, but moving a lot slower. It becomes evident that a meet may present itself. Sure enough! Just as 6747 is close enough to give a good image on the 4x5 negative, 6921 speeds into the picture from the right, going away. You trip the focal plane shutter at just the right moment and capture for all time the rare mainline meet with two steam locos! But wait a second . . . this was the old PRR. You reevaluate the setup, plot how many trains might be on the division in both directions, and you find the odds dropping very quickly! The sheer density of the traffic allowed that the meet was actually not as rare as one would think right off!! So it went on the Middle Division.

Any text offered on this division could not be complete without some mention of Denholm, Pa. Denholm was just a speck on the map, but here was the place to be in steam days. A huge timber mainline coaling plant spanned at least a dozen primary and secondary tracks at this point. Coal hoppers were spotted on top of the structure and their contents dumped into storage bins for loading into tenders of both freight and passenger locomotives. Standpipes were also handy to take water at the same time. With the advent of "Coast to Coast" tenders, and even the larger 16 wheel jobs, Denholm wharf was not used nearly as often towards the end of steam operations. But even as late as mid 1957, one could see tired and dirty 4-8-2's coaling up at the facility. Blue Ribbon passenger trains, the first runs to be dieselized, would roar under the wharf at 60 MPH kicking up coal dust from trackside and swirling it to the four winds. Several brick buildings, a pumping house, and shop stood at the right and to the east of the wharf. The only trace visible today of this once spectacular facility are the huge, dark brownstone piers that supported the structure on the left side as you look west.

There were at least four sets of track pans on the division, used for scooping water on the fly. Two of these were in partial service right to the end of steam — the pans at Hawstone and Mapleton, in the heart of the beautiful Juniata River Valley. Throw in the two-bore, three-track Spruce Creek Tunnel near Tyrone and you round out a unique piece of railroad. Incidentally, the section between Harrisburg and Lewistown, a distance of 61 Middle Division miles, was the very first portion of the fledgling PRR opened for travel and commerce on September 1, 1849. This was a full twenty years before the driving of the Golden Spike at Promontory, Utah. This section, therefore, ranks as one of the oldest original rights-of-way in the U.S.

...ing through Duncannon with train PG5 is M1 ... in the fall of 1953. The big 4-8-2 still sports her ...al footboards, rather than the customary drop ...er pilot.

Brrrr . . . it was 14 degrees above at Perdix, Pa. when Mountain 6907 sliced the chill air while toting westbound manifest out of Enola. Peter's Mountain forms the snowy backdrop for the action at Banks interlocking. January, 1955.

It seemed that nothing did more for steam photography than a cold, crystal clear, sunny day. One of my most revered shots, taken on just such a day, is this scene at Marysville, Pa. M1b 6738 holds the outside iron as she heads west while six cars back is K4s 920, due for class repairs at East Altoona.

Every once in a while, back in the mid-fifties, power hungry Pennsy would let a big "Hippo" 2-10-0 out on the Middle Division when no 4-8-2's were available. That was the case in December, 1955 when Ilsa 4594 was called upon to do her thing. Here, through Duncannon, she pounds the rails at 40 MPH with long string of empties moving west.

123

Dunncannon Doings ....

1956

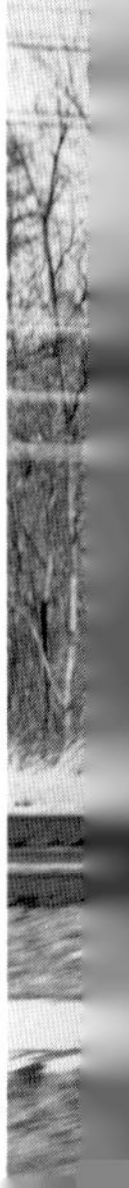

Pacing and panning the big ones on the Middle Division. Top: M1b 6744. Middle: I1 4594. Bottom: M1b 6716. All were westbound at Duncannon on three different days.

Brunswick Green Baldwin freight "Sharks" with pinstripes — ala GG1 — burble through Marysville with eastbound tonnage from Altoona. May 30, 1955.

By far the most spectacular facility on the Middle Division was the Denholm coal wharf. It was located two miles west of Mifflintown and spanned some twelve running tracks in its heyday. Those new Geep's won't be stopping here. They'll roll almost monotonously through while on their way to Enola.

4-8-2 6782 booms by double-slotted sisters 6717 and 6921 at Denholm. 6782, on PG5, will scoop water at Hawstone track pans a few miles west; the other M1's will fill up at Denholm's standpipes while taking on coal.

Denholm, Pa.
One More Time ....

A view from the top of Denholm wharf shows 6717 and 6921 blasting away from the coal-water stop in June of 1956.

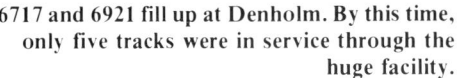

6717 and 6921 fill up at Denholm. By this time, only five tracks were in service through the huge facility.

M1b 6732, on sand, lifts coal train out of Denholm after taking coal and water (above) and heads east (below), affording the camera an exceptional view of her expansive "Coast to Coast" tender!

Two close-up looks at Pennsy's big M. Top: Left side to 3rd drivers of 6779 showing lubricator, feedwater heater pump, valve gear, and air pumps. Note that center pair of drivers are blind! Bottom: 6702 shows feedwater heater behind stack, power reverse gear, and air tanks.

Hotshot PG5, PRR's daily high priority train, received 4-8-2 power right to the end of steam, mainly because they could "Pick 'em up and lay 'em down" with those 72 inch drivers. Witness 6729's gait through Duncannon while holding the passenger (outside) westbound iron!

Now, if you please, a straight M1 (ou delivery pipes, etc.) with passenger slatted pilot but with original headligh generator positions reversed! Firema crossed the deck of 6861 to watch ca action with engineer as long train of heads west at Newpor

"Covered Wagons" wind their way through the beautiful Juniata River Valley at Mapleton, Pa. Westbound tonnage is en route from Enola to Altoona and points west.

Westbound GP9's, four of them to be exact, pass the Hawstone pumping station. Pans had been removed from outside track while eastbound passenger tanks were dry. Only center two tracks were in service for taking water on the fly. June, '56.

holds the outside iron, as engineer
not bother to scoop water at Mapletown
ghs. M1 6979 does the honors.

6738 with lowered scoop replenishes
while westbound at Hawstone. Unbe-
bly, this was 1956!

Baldwin Centipedes on westbound tonnage nearing Huntingdon, Pa.

E8's on M&E train out of Harrisburg boom through Lewistown in June, '56.

F7's in A-B-B-A multiple headed by
pass Port Interlocking, Newport, Pa.
eastbound man

Another example of Pennsy's finest in steam: M1 6979 drifts toward restrictive home signal near View Interlocking. White feather from pops shows she's about ready to lift-off.

F7's on eastbound merchandiser head into Spruce Creek tunnel near Tyrone.

One more time! PG5 behind M1 4-8-2 6907 says it all: Here is the big time East the way you like to remember it. An apt way, indeed, to close the books on the old Middle Division.

Chapter VII
Altoona & West

ALTOONA! The mystical, magical Mecca of steam! This is where Pennsy "put it all together" . . . literally and figuratively! Starting with the East Altoona enginehouse, reputed to be the world's largest. The structure was a complete 360 degree circle encompassing some 60 stalls, a foundry, and machine shop. Just to the east of the house stood the huge concrete coaling stage surrounded by myriads of storage and ready tracks for both east and westbound operations. On the occasion of my first visit in 1953, it was indeed still a true Mecca for steam. They say you never saw the full, bright rays of the sun in Altoona because of the dense smoke pall that constantly hung over the city. It is not my intention to go into a historical monologue about the city and its shops, yards, and other railroad operations. It has all been said before, many times over. The foregoing description of the East Altoona spread is related simply because it was still operational in the fifties. Despite the fact that heavy repairs were still handled there, the famed Altoona Works was already a ghost of its former self, having outshopped its final steam locomotive some six years previous. The Altoona complex, known as the largest rail facility in the world, was indeed still awesome to the wide-eye newcomer in 1953. It remained awesome even in 1960, as the photos taken from East Altoona Bridge show, during the Trainmen's strike that year.

Of course it is old news that seven miles west of Altoona, on the eastern slope of the Allegheny Mountains, lay the world's most famous railroad landmark . . . Horseshoe Curve. Here again, it would be a waste of written word and space to chortle the grandeur and mystique of the curve. Suffice to say my trip on train TT1, as related in chapter one, took on a whole new dimension as we worked upgrade out of Altoona behind six GP9's. Around the curve in fog and sleet, I must say that K4 1361 looked a lot different from TT1's cabin than she did from the trackside park!

Pittsburgh was much like Philadelphia and Harrisburg to the itinerant steam hungry photographer in the mid-fifties. Outside of rolling through the city aboard the "Broadway" or "General", (and not forgetting TT1), only one other "on the ground" trip found Pittsburgh on the itinerary.

Out in Ohio it was another story. Giant J1 2-10-4's were still hauling the black diamonds from the West Virginia coal fields for lake shipment at Sandusky, O. The single track Columbus-Sandusky run, now part of N&W, afforded the last long look at the finest steam power ever outshopped by PRR that was not cast in the mold of standard Pennsy patterns. Rather, they were constructed from borrowed blueprints of existing power (C&O) because of war time priorities and limitations. The flat Ohio profile was a complete turnabout for these engines which were more accustomed to working their guts out on the rugged Pittsburgh Division, and their flight north toward the lake port was almost effortless, even with 140 car trains! Many an interesting meet took place at the tiny interlocking at Attica Jct., Ohio, where the PRR line bisected the B&O main out of Willard. B&O Mountains and Pacifics, along with a 2-10-2 here and there, would flash by the waiting J1 or Santa Fe 2-10-4 (leased in the summer of 1956). At Sandusky, a few chunky H10 2-8-0's could be found working the tracks in and around the port, a completely satisfying compliment to the bigger road power. The J1's stayed until the fall of 1957, when, like other PRR steam power lucky enough to have survived that long, their fires were dropped when Pennsy declared enough diesels available for pool power system wide . . .

6401 and M1 6921 pose near East Altoona's ge concrete coaling stage.

M1 6888 on East Altoona enginehouse turntable in 1956. Note B8 saddle-tanker at left.

East Altoona ready track line up in 195... The cinders from some 10,000 locos ov... the span of 100 years make the groun... feel as if you were walking on a sandy beach

Two huge J1 2-10-4's pause near Rose Tower before picking up westbound tonnage. Within the hour they will do battle with Horseshoe Curve's 1.7% grade and 9 degree curve.

East Altoona ready track in August, 1955. The shop building can be seen between the two locomotives, while part of the world's largest roundhouse is visible just aft of 6729's tank.

B8 saddletank shop switcher hauls dead 2-10-0 across the table at East Altoona roundhouse.

For one who arrived on the scene a year or two after the T1 Duplexes were retired, this photographic impression of 4-4-4-4 5546 is a memorable one. Here is a magnificent machine reduced to almost rubble in her tracks. The mighty did indeed fall!

East Altoona - 1960

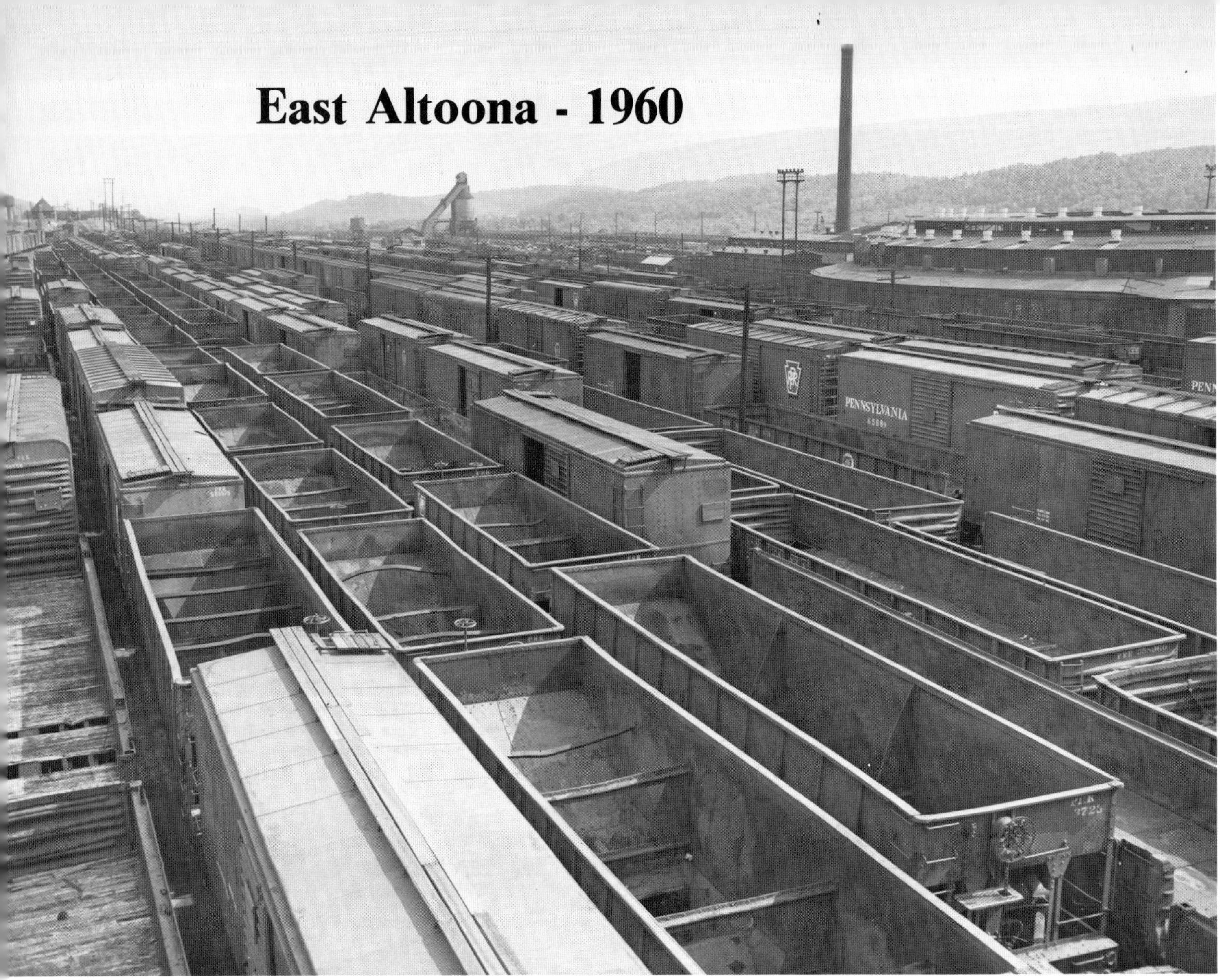

An almost unbelievable scene at East Altoona looking from the first overbridge. Yards and main tracks are clogged with strikebound cars in 1960. Steam facilities at rear were razed in 1968.

View looking west from same bridge shows tie-up of diesels and cabin cars during the short Trainmen's strike.

Close associate and diesel expert Tony Organek tells me there are at least 17 varieties of growlers in this one shot. Altoona in the strike of 1960.

TT1 rolls around Horseshoe in sleet, snow, and fog while the author was on the memorable assignment for TRAINS Magazine. Even old friend 1361 on display in the park seems to be huddled up against the elements!

The weather was a bit more respectable at the curve when 1361 posed in the summer of 1958.

E8's roll eastbound through Allegheny Tunnel at Gallitzin. Stone inset at apex of tunnel bore reads: "1890" "Wm. M. Brown, Chief Engineer" "W. R. Michie, Assistant Engineer" "F. H. Clement & Co., Contractors".

Linestone about to roll across the Monongahela River as Port Perry branch freight out of Turtle Creek heads for Pittsburgh. Union R.R. bridge is at right. Tracks in foreground are P&LE and B&O.

TT1 pulls into Pittsburgh's Island Avenue Yards. The TOFC train out of Kearny, N.J. has a Chicago appointment in 15 hours.

2-10-4 6403 bears down on rural grade crossing near Bellevue, Ohio while on Columbus-Sandusky run. Every time I look at this shot, I have to question whether or not I would get this close to the action if the opportunity should again present itself. The photo, 18 years removed by the time this is in print, is sobering, to say the least!

Coal destined for lake shipment from the Ohio port of Sandusky rolls through the flatlands behind J1 6484. Action is north of Attica Jct.

Doubleheaded 2-10-4's pass water tank at Sandusky with a caboose hop for Columbus.

2 big "J's" in the hole near Lima, Ohio in 1956. Pennsy's 2-10-4 erected from C&O plans, turned out to be the road's best modern steam power, outlasting duplexes and experimentals.

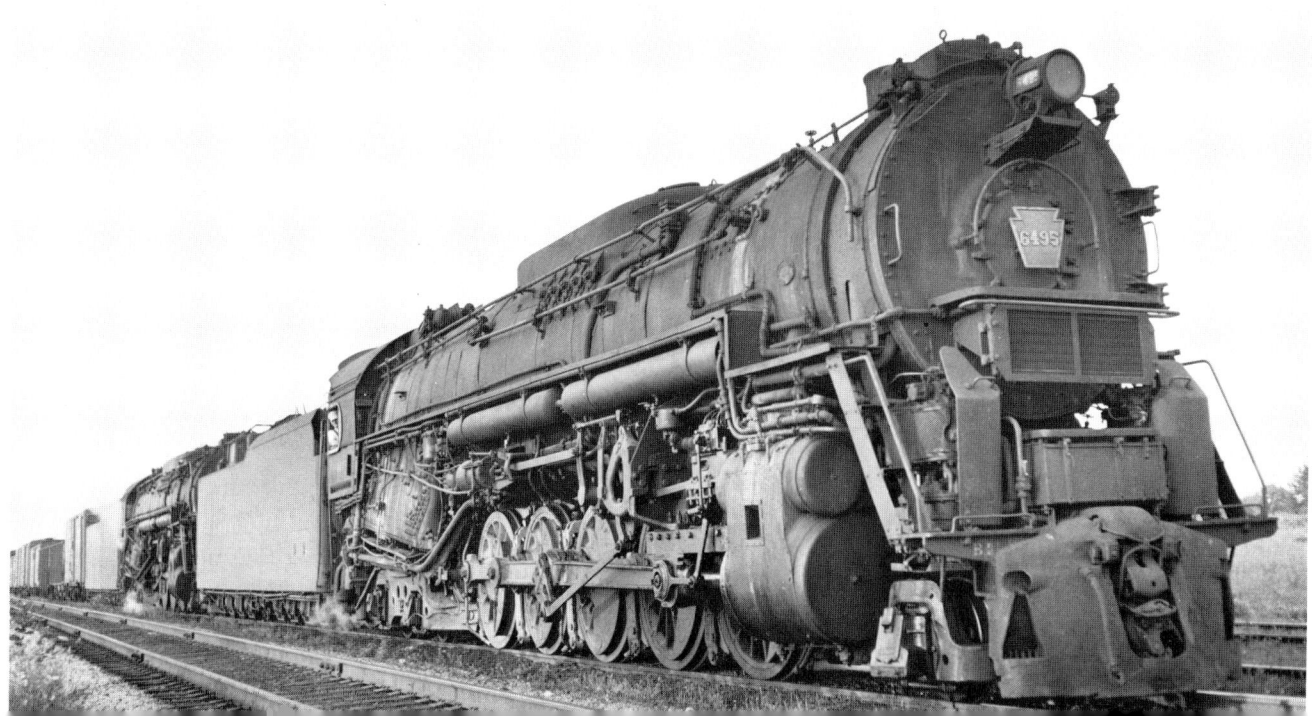

They did things differently on Lines West: H10 8173, working the Sandusky port area, had gracefully curved coal boards, and retained her old, big headlight in its original position along with the big "claw" pilot beam mounted marker lights!

J1 6484 is framed in the doorway of the smallish enginehouse at Sandusky in 1956.

Talk about discoveries: A first visit to Northumberland enginehouse in 1953 provided this view of D16sb 1223. The famous 4-4-0 was protected by a tarpaulin that had to be rolled back before this flash shot could be recorded. 1223, of course, is now operated by Strasburg Railroad.

Chapter VIII
L C L (Less than Chapter Lots)

As the title of this chapter would indicate, a few items that did not easily find a niche in any of the preceding chapters come home to roost here. For example, the "Great Locomotive Hoax, Installment 2", concerning 1737-3750 switcheroo ala 7002. Then we have things like the last K4 fan trip, some human interest photography, and the latest diesels that would ever wear a Pennsylvania Railroad Keystone. Also, a few shots of the existing locomotives that are now in the Pennsylvania State Museum at Strasburg. M1 6755 looks as though a good fire on her grates would be all she'd need to reach out once again for the feel of the High Iron she once ruled!

Several hours after she became the first of the "modern" locos to be refurbished by PRR for their historical collection, A5s 94 posed outside Northumberland enginehouse. Note the live steam in the background. This was 1955!

The Great Locomotive Hoax -- Part 2!

Above: the original 1737, deteriorated beyond reasonable repair, in preservation line at "Nory". Below: Eureka! 1737 with a face lift? Wrong; that's 1737's number plate affixed to the smoke box of 3750! Right, bottom, next page: 3750 with her own plate while in service at Bay Head Jct., N.J.

Years ago, when PRR first became historically minded, some eager PR man thought that maybe the big road should preserve Speed Queen Atlantic 7002, which had set an all time steam speed mark of 127.1 MPH way back in 1905. Now, the original 7002, an E7, had been cut up in the early 1930's, so Pennsy latched onto one of the few remaining E3's and decked her out as the original pace setting 4-4-2! It did not take the faithful long to reason out the hoax, and it has been laughed about over many years. This should not be misconstrued as a complaint; after all, an E3 was saved and that was something! The renumbered 7002 reposes today at the State Museum at Strasburg.

Now we come to 1957, when PRR was phasing out the last of its in-service steam power. They brought out the original 1914 K4, number 1737, and sent her to Northumberland for refurbishing along with other notables of the steam era. She was in such poor condition that an appraisal showed her to be too far gone for anything but a 100% rebuilding job. But wait a minute ... PRR had at least 35 K4's that were in excellent condition ... why not renumber a good one while nobody's looking and cut up the relic. Well, lightning struck twice ... K4s 3750 became K4s 1737, and once again, no one was fooled! But we did get a good K4 in place of a shell. It is my understanding that in the State Museum, 3750 will get her old number back, and 1737's number plate will be retired with dignity! Thus ends part two of the great locomotive hoax!

3750 roars toward camera with North Jersey Coast train in the spring of 1957.

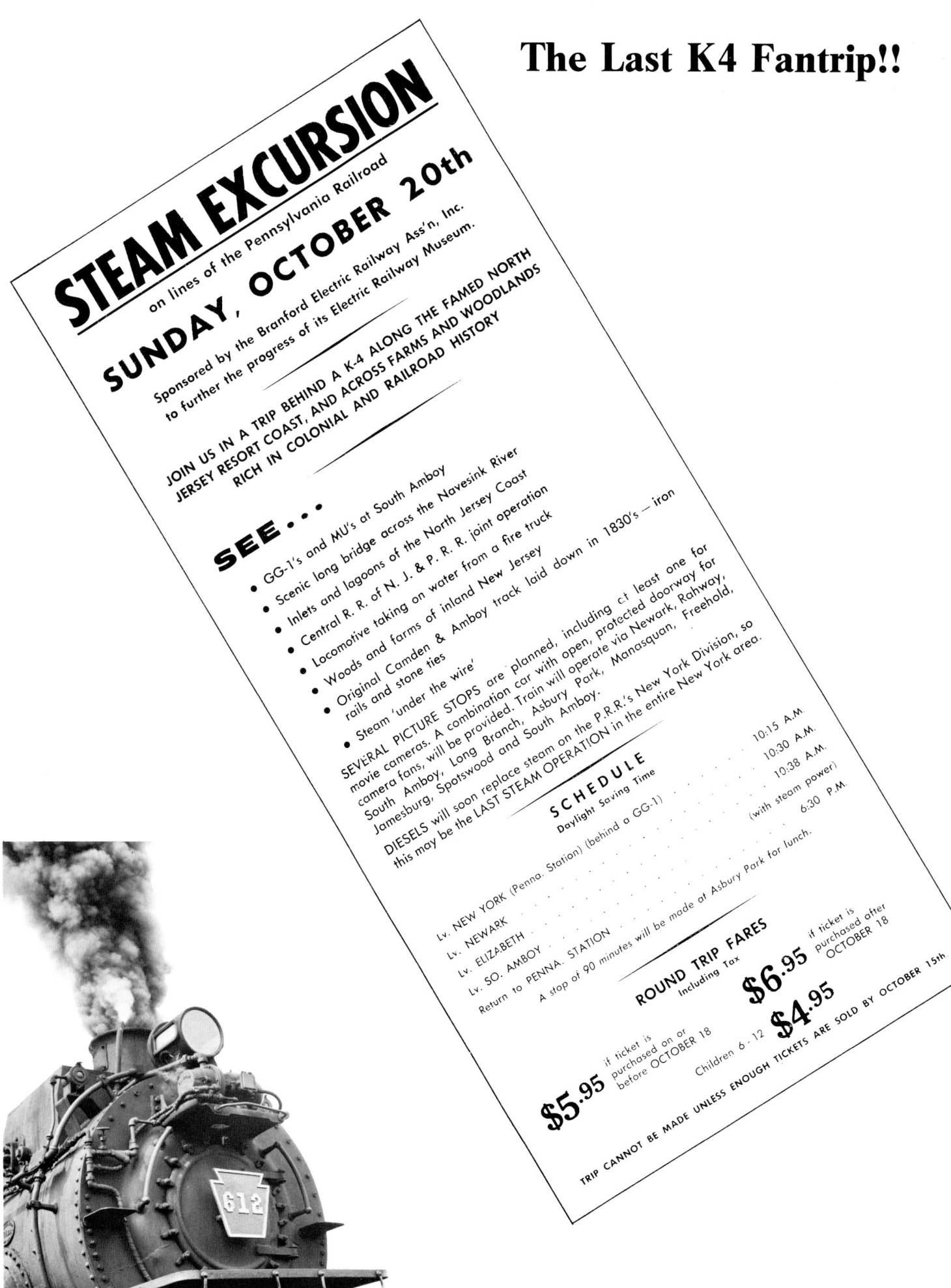

Old 612 with Charles Hess at the throttle, Billy Van Dyke on the left hand side, rolls final K4 fan trip of October 20, 1957 near Jamesburg, N.J. 612 also made last steam run in regular service on NY&LB less than a month later.

Meet a few of the boys who kept the old K4's running at South Amboy.

Engineer Andy Fountain, right, and his regular fireman Johnny Maxwell, center, pose with their favorite K4 and a young fellow by the name of Don Wood!

My two favorite K4's look into the bright morning sun at Bay Head Junction, N.J.

Contrasts: The last M1 4-8-2, 6755, and new SD40 6100.

Acknowledgments

Outwardly, it is apparent that the reader could misconstrue this work as a one man show. The fact that it was conceived, written, illustrated and designed by the author is only one facet of a considerably complex project. Anyone associated with the printing and publishing business will be quick to point out that presenting only the above would leave one far short of the finished, printed product. For example, my notoriously bad spelling and grammar was put to the test by my good friend and close associate Tony Organek. Tony was also at hand while layout and design were in progress, helping avoid the myriad pitfalls and the commiting of errors both of omission and commission! He was ably backed up by Railroader-Railbuff-typist Roman Sohor. Between the three of us, hopefully, most of the wrongs have been righted! Messrs Organek and Sohor began their rail hobbies with the coming of the diesel age, and have been entrusted with terminology, model numbers, etc., where internal combustion locomotives are concerned. Any shortcomings in these areas are the sole responsibility of these gentlemen! In all seriousness, without the help of these two contributors, I REMEMBER PENNSY would have been a lot longer in reaching publication, and I remain forever in their debt because of it.

Equally important is the contribution of long time friend and associate Carl H. Sturner. Carl had the foresight and the desire to see this book become a reality. So much so, that his outlet, AUDIO-VISUAL DESIGNS, has backed and published the work.

A special word of thanks is in order for Mr. Don Derrick who guides the fortunes of Compton Press. His patience and understanding as well as his close watch on the project from inception to completion provided much encouragement while in the throes of production. The quality of the finished volume should speak loudly for Don and his craftsmen in Morristown, N.J.

In conclusion, a word for the late George W. (Bud) Rothaar. Many of my early rail photo safaris were made in the company of Rothaar and casual acquaintance Gene Gentsch. Bud was as dedicated a train watcher (PRR, of course) and student of Pennsy motive power that ever came along. He was at the wheel of the auto used on most of the M1 pacing photos in the Middle and Susquehanna Division chapters. As it was to turn out, our courses veered in time, and viewpoints became sharply divided on a number of fronts during the mid-fifties. We didn't communicate at all in the 17 years preceeding the tragic accident of last winter which took the life of his mother and eventually resulted in his passing. I thought it only right that his name be between the covers of a book on his beloved Pennsylvania. I must also admit to being disappointed with myself in that I would never have thought of including the name Bud Rothaar had I not been told of his death . . .

Sincerely,

Among the last delivered power to wear the proud Pennsy Keystone were GM SD45's, delivered in late 1967 and early '68. 6184 poses outside Enola diesel shop.

The grand old lady of the rails, the classic GG1 electric in her most attractive dress. 4895 at South Amboy, N.J. in 1954.